Too Bright to See

Too Bright to See

Poems

DAVID BOOTH

SIMI
PRESS

Printed in the United States of America

ISBN 978-1-7341142-6-3

Some of the poems in this collection were first published in
the Washington Square Review, The Farallon Review, Quick
Fiction, Absomaly, Sudden Stories: The Mammoth Book of
Miniscule Fiction, and Simi Press Magazine.

Simi Press
www.simipress.com

For Ingrid

CONTENTS

APPROPRIATE KISS

I'd never kissed a cop before and when I did it was like a regular kiss but with a loaded story behind it. She didn't know I knew her profession but had left her badge lying open on the table. What she did for a living had nothing to do with our curiosity about each other. So we French kissed. I want to say it was nothing special. It was neither special nor unpleasant. It would have gotten better with practice, but our hearts weren't in it. It hardly seems worth mentioning that I'd never kissed a cop before, except that it brought to mind an objective fact about my upbringing. I have no memory of my father ever having given me an appropriate kiss. Not once on the cheek. Not once on the forehead. Never on the mouth that I can remember. Nor did he hug me or say I love you. He may have ruffled my hair a little from time to time, but I don't think so. I think he had a total aversion to touch. If this is a loaded story it is not sad to me. That I've never kissed my father, or him me, may be a quite significant story about individual human capacity that I may or may not wish to delve into, but either way it holds no meaning for me in my life.

SUNFLOWER

When a man's much older husband
begins to convalesce
he takes a lover
someone close to his age
and the two of them
the new lovers
tend to the needs
of a dying man
their elder

A WORLD WITHOUT CARS

With birthdays but a year and a day apart, and she the elder and young for her age, and he the younger whose turns of phrase grow frankly repetitive, they'd eaten beef in the early days of their joint celebration and across sinewy time, when bodies gray with food beliefs greening, of the baby spinach and veggie lasagna they swore up and down to savor, they left bites on their plates and their stomachs a quarter empty in an inner and outer show of moderation. Pressing her cheek to his to blow out candles one day in their fifties, she wished to herself to feel happy and fulfilled at the time of her death. Like planning a wedding, she arranged the flowers in her head and the ones before them that make the best centerpieces for birthday dinners. He wished that the movie they were seeing later that night would be at least a little entertaining. It was to be a hundred-minute car chase broken up by scenes from the childhoods of the chasers and those chased, as if so many turning points from the deep pasts of so many passengers could justify such a hair-raising event as two cars careening down the highway with little regard for the safety of others. It was after all a hot day and the gist of the chase, like an old-time feud, involved an ancient wound, an insult like a family heirloom, about somebody's mother that cut to the core of a man's need to strut his stuff with his chest thrust forward and balls of fist hung like unused mallets. Childhoods aside, the funny part of the chase was the fact that every time the chased sped up, the chaser sped up, and every time the chased slowed down, the chaser slowed down, so that the distance between them remained constant. As you may have

3

guessed, you must suspend your disbelief when it comes to the guzzling of gas. Chalk it up to that six-shooter that in the movies shoots a hundred rounds or more. No one is stopping to reload and underneath it all everyone cares about everyone immensely.

TO DRIVE THIS MIRACLE OUT OF EXISTENCE

Some people enjoy the taste of Miracle Burgers. We speak now of the ahimsa crowd, that doesn't wear a single strand of cow leather, let alone cook a goose, swat a fly, or eat raw honey. A Miracle Burger is a meatless food item that tastes like venison. Its critics call it 'an ultra-processed junk food.' They wish to devalue, to de-popularize, and ultimately to drive it out of existence. They will do so, they claim, via a relentless word-of-mouth campaign. It doesn't matter, though, if in fact it does taste like the real thing. If it's delicious, nothing they can do will make a difference.

CALENDAE

The year of the horse
            is an action poem
so seize your subject matter by the mane
                & ride it/write quick!
                  The animal of the year
                        of my own birth
                  the monkey
        of popular imagination
      many find agile
    if not a bit mischievous
  I find at its worst
a royal pain
      at its best other-
          worldly

      always landing on its feet
         somewhere between
           not much to look at
            & yes, handsome.

But this is not what I meant to say.
      What I meant to say
         was will you go out with me?

A TRIUMPH WAS A PUBLIC SHOW

[Reading Shakespeare while sheltering in place]

Saturday noon finds eight friends gathered virtually for a read-around of *A Midsummer Night's Dream*. I am one of them. I'm always one. This circle is the one I've belonged to the longest. At sixty, our host Alan is ten years older than I am and taking our sheltering period to grow the long free beard he'd craved wearing as a child. He strokes it. He sits beside his wife Rachel in their loveseat flanked by antique lampshades. It's good to see them. It's good to see everybody—Stacy, Pauline, Ransom, Mel, Jay, Bernard, Erica, and Sandy—looking so healthy. We live in California, North Carolina, Chicago, Albuquerque, and London. Masks may hang from our necks but again we are healthy. Everyone's hair is longer. Looking past their smiling faces on my computer screen, I'm drawn to incidentals:

...spines of books about anthropology, cooking, umbrella handle, tidiness, a painting of a squirrel in a tree of Chinese lettering, weariness, chaos, autumnal colors red and golden, minimalist, business as usual, shabby chic, framed certificates of achievement, framed elders, children, transitional look, mad scientist, a pot of ivy hanging in macramé, rustic, clay figurine silhouetted in bright window, industrial look, a cat walks across a keyboard, Frank sets his laptop on his piano, contemporary, Jay's wife poking her head in to say hi, mid-century modern credenza; a stray toddler (Little Gregory) cooing as he passes....

We curate our frames. Everyone wants us to see something. An object. A quality. My guitar hangs on the wall behind me. I have placed such worn titles as Merton's *Conjectures of a Guilty Bystander* and Shirky's *Here Comes Everybody* in plain view for anyone who's looking.

Drawing my name from a hat, Alan assigns me the roles of Theseus, the Duke Athens, and Oberon, King of the Fairies. They're both men, though Shakespeare's fairies are hermaphrodites in my memory of them. Both lead their minions, an earthly troop in chain mail and swordplay on one hand and, on the other, a band of spirits, Peasblossom, Moth, and Cobweb among them. I want to say that Theseus is doctrinaire, bound up with fear, and that Oberon is a noble and supportive guy who will drug his wife with magic to steal the changeling. The play is a comedy.

Playing the parts of Helena and Hermia, our London friends Stacy and Pauline reintroduce us to their eleven-and-a-half-year-old daughter Caitlin. In her pajamas, she's dragged her blanket into the frame on her way to beddy-bye. I met her once when she was an infant and again a year ago. She'd recently heard that old-fashioned phrase, 'If such-and-such happens, *I'll eat my hat.*' It was like a song stuck in her head that she kept singing: 'If Mom's on time, I'll eat my hat.' 'I'll eat my hat if there aren't a million people already waiting.' 'I'll eat my hat if I need my dumb coat after all.' I remember feeling charmed by this, and also a little jealous. To be in the newness of it all! I told a story called 'The Hat Eaters' in her honor. It was about all of us. Everyone roundly panned it as satire that was less a piece of social commentary and more a laundry list of my own personal grievances. I've always felt this was an overreaction. But that's not important either. What's important is that we all have our parts to play. If I know this crowd we will read loudly and softly and with gusto. We will modulate our voices.

My copy of *A Midsummer Night's Dream* comes from an anthology published in Cleveland in 1925 by the World Syndicate Company. It belonged to my late grandmother on my father's side and includes all the Bard's comedies. Its faux leather cover hangs by a thread. The printers have included the phrase 'A triumph was a public show' in a distinct font in the bottom margin of the first page of the play. These words are not part of the script. Appearing nowhere else in the volume, they feel more poignant than practical. The more times I read them the more they sound like an incantation. And why the past tense? But this too is beside the point. We're all online together, and it's time to start. I clear my throat and say to my friends in a fairly flat voice, 'Now, fair Hippolyta, our nuptial hour draws on apace....' This is my Theseus. This is my Oberon.

[Clover]

Girls, she said, have the worst lives ever.
Boys have it much easier.

First of all
—she counted on her forefinger—
the *crushes*.
Everyone around you is dating
and the one time you do
you feel like a total moron.

Second
—she counted on her middle finger—
everyone else is *suave* and *smooth*

9

and you don't know what to do
with your chest
your thighs
let alone your toes and fingers.

Thirdly
—she bent back her ring finger
like peeling a banana—
everything freaks you out.
The stupidest thing makes you
well up inside yourself.
There's just so much energy.

But the worst part by *far*
is the whole learning about things.
When you're a kid
you're adorable.
Then all of a sudden
you're not a little girl anymore
and you have to learn
how to act and talk.
You feel like a clumsy animal.

So you invent a girl named Clover
a mix between a regular Mary Sue
and a princess out of your Middle-
Earthen imagination
and cast her in your redo
of *A Midsummer Night's Dream*
an old play in your own new style
strained with similes
thought

[Clover]

Though she's never met a person
smarter than herself
she must concede
that she's never liked or loved anyone
who didn't have a genius of her own.
In accessorizing her intelligence
she wears summer dresses in the
    summer
and of the flowers she admires
sometimes she plucks one
and sets it in her hair
before taking a walk through town.
If in private she thinks herself a little
    ugly
if in private she fights tooth and nail
against every little gray hair
and the weight she's gaining
she nevertheless has an insatiable
    sexual appetite
that the men along the lane
would give anything to help satisfy.
In her mind/in the meantime
she practices the conversations they'd
    have
if ever she felt motivated to talk to one
    of them.

A woman assumed
to be a man
asked a younger woman
presumably
(judging from eyes and curls)
her daughter
to please not be
a Pollyanna.

10

bursts
lines that lengthen out and draw back in again
like those drawn for an electroencephalogram
while I'm sleeping.

This time Puck meets Clover at a wedding
and falls madly in love.
Titania forbids the two lovers
 from seeing each other
 but they don't listen.
Only the old hag finds out
and makes Oberon force Puck
either to dump Clover or to get fired.

Puck goes to work at an In 'n' Out Burger
on the interstate between Modesto and Visalia
when Oberon shows up for lunch
promising that Titania has relaxed
and will let him date Clover.

Does Puck forgive them
and start his old life over again?
I can't decide.
I'm not sure if people
ever really go back to the old situation
even in predictable fictions like this one.
I'll have to sit with it for a while
and, you know,
let it percolate.

Nay, faith,
let me not
play a woman;
I have a beard coming.

[Flute's reaction once as-
signed the part of Thisbe.]

TAMIR (I WISH I WERE A PSALM)

A

Instructions: Read and annotate the paragraph below. When you are finished, go back and 1) put one line under the subject of each sentence, 2) put two lines under the predicate of each sentence, and 3) bracket the objects.

In the middle of the twentieth century two million blacks migrated from the South to northern and western cities to get away from Jim Crow. Many were met with racist white violence in their new safer places, call them homes. Chicago comes to mind from my memory of the play by Lorraine Hansberry that I read and saw performed on a no longer extant proscenium stage when I was fifteen. Supported by progressive black and white activists, some schools in those days did moral combat against racism by instituting Intercultural Education. It's hard to say it wasn't a good idea. Then we hear the NAACP criticizing songs taught in music classes that use the words "darky" and the most famous and most proprietary word of all, which is not a word for God but the n-word. Words feel most loaded that insinuate and engender a maximum number of oppressors. Then arose the question of what to do with history books in praise of the KKK keeping "foolish Negros" out of government. Then some people wanted to know, "Why must my child read about Little Black Sambo at school?" Even Race Liberals of certain times and places [call it an epoch and approximate the size of it] argued that textbooks can't influence prejudice even if a classroom is a seedbed for dissemination. Black activists must have been seen as hypersensitive in those days. Back in the day defenders of a status quo must have asked over and over again, "Where's your proof of this?"

B

Once a toy makes it to the table, the head of the household perched at the head of the table proclaims squirt guns *off limits* at mealtime. Behold his cowl of soft gray hair. A pale flesh pot of blue irises and gun to bring him back to a day when, craving Band-Aids and skeleton keys, he made midwinter flyovers in a rubber-band-propelled helicopter. Gun brings him home to days of craving when the air was gray and clouds muted the sun's rays, and he monitored from on high the comings and goings at his sister's dollhouse with the whirlybird he called Peacekeeper. The smell of the gun gives rise to summer when sunshine acts on plastic to warm the grassy water inside. A barefooted boy breaks from a grove of trees and running from lawn to lawn to meet the enfilade head-on reloads at a neighbor's spigot. The reverie ends with a report from Cleveland in 2014.

> *There's a guy here with a pistol.*
> *You know it's probably fake,*
> *but he's pointing it at everybody.*

An airsoft pistol is a facsimile weapon indistinguishable from the genuine article.

> *There's a black male on the swings…*
> *he keeps pulling a gun out of his pants*
> *and pointing it at people.*

In a dinnertime prayer for Tamir, the head of the household says of his own safe son, "May all boys be psalms sung before guns get drawn."

C

The laddies learned what they learned about race relations from the books they read in school and lessons learned from their cunning instructors. It was also all over the media.

COVIDAVID

A sixth grader asks her teacher is it okay to have a good day while others are suffering. Before he can answer, her peers shout into mics like shouts in a brick-and-mortar classroom. Their faces light up his viewscreen. Voices draw down the tedium of sheltering. 'Be happy about your happiness,' they try to tell each other, 'cognizant of the world happening around you.' He doesn't change the subject so much as its direction, when he asks, 'What's one thing you'd like to do when life returns to normal?' The lists they make start small and grow increasingly unrealistic.

STILL LIFE WITH SMOKERS

How many times have I ashed a shoe or smoked a poem or talked loudly on the other shoe on a crowded bus at noon, as if what I had to say was everyone's primary interest? I'm sorry. I thank you for your own discretion. You are my role model of the public sphere. I'm not being sarcastic when I say this, even if my tone of voice tells a different story.

I want to do a still life of a poet, an ashtray, and a woman's tennis shoe, but it's the same every time. The poet can't sit still for the picture. His curiosity about who the shoe belongs to leads him around the room when the name of the game is stillness. So no still life for the time being, unless I alter my vision to exclude the poet. The problem is that he's my best friend in the city and near the top of my list for all times and places.

A tennis shoe is a wonderful thing to wear on and off the court. It makes me feel nimble. Quick like the player I was once when I was twenty. Then I was a smoker for twenty years, and the very thought of a full-length match took my breath away. I smoked to be in the image of a poet. One day the greatest poet I personally know asked me to please stop smoking. 'But you smoke,' I reminded him. 'Kind of a double standard, don't you think?' 'I'd like you to be around,' he said, 'for as long as possible.'

This morning I bought an ashtray for a poet friend of mine. The irony of the object lay in its shape of a tennis shoe. It sits before me now, beside a flowerpot and an apple. It's ironic because our lungs, his and mine together, now that we're both ex-smokers, are as pink as they'll ever be. Before meeting him to hand off his present, I do as he would do and stop to write a poem. It's a love poem about First Love. Because it must accomplish a lot to mean much to someone who doesn't know me, it sets me up for failure. In it, I must do the following:

CLIMBING UP

fying"
more terri-
makes it much
Your feeling foolish
don't call yourself a fool.
to help you. If you do, please
I fear you'll fall when I'm not here
"We all fall from time to time, Mom.
she remembers her daughter's response:
self up off the steps to continue climbing,
her daughter. Watching Gem now pick her-
"Sometimes when I fall I feel like a fool," she'd told
stumbled recently. At her age, it could have been worse.
What mother can bear to see her child fall? She herself had
When her daughter stumbles on the steps, she feels just awful.

ONE PERFECT ROSE

For Phil Doub

If roses won't prove fatal to write about, wilt they must with pleadings set with idyllic settings. You can't always see this coming, a biochemical response beyond naming, a nameless byproduct characterized by falling up and swooning. It's not like it kicks up any dust or anything, or sounds an alarm like a panicked conversation, arriving both early and often to drive the unsentimental crazy.

I may not be as practical as I sound. Yesterday I went looking for the answer to a question I couldn't formulate. It went something like, 'What is wrong with me?' In contrast, today is the day of days, the most wonderful I've ever lived through. It's been a long time since I worked with my shirt off in the hot sun. I'm planting dwarf roses around stone walkways. Climbing ones over trellised arches. Note the care I take to prune back the element that makes a comedy romantic. It's worth it even if all romance is hilarious. If my aversion here makes me giggle condescendingly, let me at least informally acknowledge your love of sap as an incredible source of power. But this is about science, man, and the Old Enologists who for centuries now have lived and worked up the road from here. Everyone knows the trick they play, for me a perpetual revelation: In fashioning an early warning system against sharpshooters and bunch rot, encircle your grapevines with ever-blooming roses of the same pH and watch for critters getting after them.

See this rose here. It's yours for a dollar. You may ask, 'Why would I pay a perfect stranger a dollar for a rose growing in my own garden?' See that one there, the one spilling into the one you have your eye on? Before I knocked on your door, I plucked an even prettier one and sold it to your neighbor for a fiver. You get the discount for owning the bushes in the first place. You may ask, 'Why would my neighbor give a perfect stranger five dollars for a rose out of my garden?'

One, these are beautiful flowers and, like a game of hide and go seek, it is the nature of things. Two, their scents, nasturtium, orrisroot, apple, clove, lemon, are things out of nature. Three, in our love of reds, pinks, and yellows, some splotched ones occur naturally in the wild. Four, what appear to us as our reds, pinks, and yellows may look different to pollinators. Five is my hunch that, with the obvious exception of the sky, blue doesn't happen as naturally in the wild as other hues do. Six, nowhere in the Bible, the Rig Veda, the Zend-Avesta, or the Homeric poems is the sky called blue or its color even noted. One wonders if they ever looked up or, if they did, what color they saw. Seven, it's a hot enough day for sweat to soak through from our armpits. Eight, kids are playing air hockey in the air-conditioned basement and roller hockey on the hot asphalt one street over. Nine: smell of grass clippings. Ten: chit-chit-chit of an old-time sprinkler system. Eleven: rubber of cars rolling over pea gravel. Twelve: wind shishing in treetops. Thirteen, the sky is blue and cloudless.

Our early warning system reminds one of the Old Miners' trick of hanging canaries in their cages in the old mines they dug. Guinea pigs running headlong into waves of carbon monoxide may give us a sense of meaning in our own lives, when April showers once brought mayflowers and roses fail for phylloxera's arrival. If ever more sensitive birds get sick before men do, any sentinel species, honey bee, bat, crayfish, swallow, may inform our Climate Change Thinking. The grand dame of resistance writing, Muriel Rukeyser, made it more urgent in *U.S. 1*, her poems from '38, when she drove to West Virginia to record a wife saying: 'I first discovered what was killing these men.' Their labor was subterranean whose reverse alchemy took them away from gold into the business of carbon. Said the doctors at the time, 'Miner's phthisis, fibroid phthisis, / grinder's rot, potter's rot, / whatever it used to be called, / these men did not want to die.' So we must answer yes to the question of whether or not silicosis is an occupational disease or a hazard.

The Old Enologists arrived here from Transcaucasia and Asia Minor with pit stops at the Fertile Crescent and the Nile Delta. 'Hello Franschhoek,' they said. And 'Howdy' to Kakheti, Istria, Valle de Guadalupe, Sherry Triangle, and Colchagua. And 'Hi' to Alsace. And 'How do you do, Porto?' They soon had everyone driving pests away from their vines and flavoring the wines of a not-so- distant future by amassing clumps of rosemary and lavender around the shanks of rosebushes. This was about the time I found a faience cup in the California loam with a chip like a bite taken out of it. It beamed not the name of a pharaoh but that of a far distant rancher.

'The unfortunate need of words,' I tried explaining to everyone. My most obvious emendations were the addition of words, half a dozen big ones plunked down in the middle of a plainspoken elegy, to arrest the attention of the departing dead, John Rutherford, in case he clung to his love of stilted language throughout his transition to the afterlife. In case he clung to sarcasm, I put that in, too. Insult? One or two searing ones. Wordplay? The best I could manage. Practical jokes? I couldn't think of one in time. Like Shakespeare's least famous fools, he never caught his own malapropisms, when opinioned is pinioned, odorous is odious, and vigitant is vigilant, so I packed them, that he might hear his own flawless diction one more time. Though he was never a churchgoer he believed in the function of God in his increasingly secular community. Explain that one to me. In any event, I can see him now, carried up the hill head-up by celestial children. Soon after their departure, the roses in his garden surrendered to convolvuluses.

Finally, the story I was meant to tell could be the trailer of a feature length movie. As sick to my stomach as it makes me to say this, for the best effect, read by rose-light from the penumbra of high personal pathos: *He loved her even after she left with that man of hers. He loved her today. He loved her yesterday. He would always love her. When that man of hers died, he cried for her, and he cried. A different she loved a different he, even after he left with that woman of his. She loved him today. She loved him yesterday. She would love him forever. When his woman died, she cried for him, and she cried. They've known each other for a few weeks now. They remind each other of the men and women they didn't go with. They make love in the afternoon, at lunchtime, when their spouses are away and the house is filled with daylight.* There are funny parts, too. The funny parts come later. They bring us into a time when everyone looks visibly older.

GENTILE READERS

Two young friends read a single book at the same time, together. One of them sits at a table while the other stands behind him, reading over his shoulder. The problem is that the one who is sitting is both a much faster reader and the one who turns the pages. The problem is solved without a word spoken. The one sitting rereads passages, while the slower of the two, so as to match his friend's pace exactly, only pretends he is reading. He prefers the closeness of his friend to the unfolding story.

NERVES

On opening day a boy much too young to be smoking tosses his half-smoked cigarette into a trashcan and enters the building. Once inside, he takes the elevator to the top floor, where everyone is waiting. When the elevator doors finally open, he heads straight for the stairwell and, running back down to where he came from, finds both the trashcan ablaze and the crowd he'd always imagined.

A NEAR TRAGEDY

Once we were back on dry ground to cheer her up I told her I had saved up enough money to buy her a present. "Well let's go buy it then," she said, and combed the salt out of her hair.

"No need," I said. I had taken the liberty of picking something out myself and was even having it delivered to her house. Delivery was actually included in the price.

When she asked me what it was, I said, "If I told you it'd hardly be a surprise, now would it?" When she asked me if she could have three guesses, I told her that she could have as many guesses as she wanted, but that she would never guess, not in a thousand years.

"It must be a high definition TV," she said next. "Is it not a high definition TV?"

"Let's not play the guessing game," I answered, and went up from the shore without her, wondering how in the world she ever guessed and, in the moment that she did, whether or not I had kept a straight face.

TOO BRIGHT TO SEE

A boy walks in waist-high water parting and swirling back together behind him. Water gives off lapping noises when he dips his hands and raises them again like tilted ladles. Water makes going slow across an endless ocean.

Too bright to see, the distant horizon is a smattering of yellowy copper, and orange I see, with a kind of blue splashing upward. The variegated sky is as endless as the ocean. A few clouds pass over.

With an ocean coming and going at his waist, a boy walks into a sun both blinding and warm. His skin and hair are brined. He shades his eyes with hands pruning. His face catches light and his torso, catching light, flickers like a candle floating ceremoniously at daybreak.

Neither his legs nor his intellect drive him to where he's going. The water is too deep for his feet to touch bottom. Too deep for thought. Once asleep and now awakened by the sensation of being carried, he rides a submerged animal like adventurous boys with hair swept back and their own oceans' horses. In a rare moment of joy [as if the mucus collecting in his lungs could drain away once and for all and all by itself] he crosses into the rising sun straddling a hippopotamus.

THE BOOK SHE'S READING

She's reading the book
The Collaborative Habit.

it's about artists in collaboration

she's bugging me to read it with her

it's just that we're not artists

LULU'S LOVE POEM

Lulu loves his wandering eye
and not his wandering eye
        that's a lie she likes
the lustiness with which
he sometimes glances at women.

A chubby girl
with a huge head of curly red hair
        [red like cherry boucle]
reminds Lulu of Campion's depiction
of a preadolescent Janet Frame
in the biopic *An Angel At My Table*.
        Or maybe it's Frame herself
and not a filmmaker's depiction.
Yes, it's Frame, the novelist who once wrote

                I must go down to the seas again
                to find where I
                buried the hatchet with Yesterday

When someone tells you
            she adores

                   a

                t

            o

          n

        a

        l

listen   music

Self-conscious men invite punishment.
        Lulu has grown fond of reinforcing
her beau's belittlement of himself.
        Men less manly than he is
in less healthy relationships than theirs is
reify the insecurities of the women they love
so why not turn it around on them?

Sometimes Lulu believes
she was born to help others
and looks upon creation
with eyes of love.
Sometimes she holds it
in the periphery of her vision.
Sometimes she instists
it owes her *big time*
and confronts it with proverbial fists
of fury, when her all too real voice
splotches her face red
and inflames her nostrils.

Lulu's dream is to one day renounce such extremes
as coming and going
sameness and otheness
and the hold eternity and annihilation have
                              on human beings.
Such animation outstretches the day
and wrecks the one that follows.

Mistaken for a marksman,
she claims the rank of first fine shot.
So tote an empty weapon

ideologue
stranger
genesis
occasion
repose
negative capability
foggy notion
debt
ire
sonority
crimson
respiration

antithesis
routine
gesture

a wasted life
manic
midnight

and a cloth of rocks
far beyond the broad ephemeral border.

The blue green bullet behind the forehead
personalizes known landscapes.

WHAT IS DESPICABLE?

Is this a replay of the 'if it's mine it can't be worth much' gambit? That gambit I so often deploy against myself, out of a suspicion that my experience of things is compromised by some original and inexplicable flaw[?] —Harry Mathews

One sacred pedestrian says to another, "I know you don't like me, I hear it in your voice, see it in your nuanced body. I am intolerable." How embarrassing, when someone we despise appeals to our face against the sentence handed down on them.

REALM

Dear
smushed,
saddened,
creative-
type,

The words you made,
                    quiet
                            damn it
                                    kiss my ass
                                                reminder
                                        shut up
                            cuddle up
                de-meaning
            ban-ter
miss the point
all together.

Please reconsider
your position more generally
& also the possibility
of crystallizing one facet only.

Say more about what's here
than what's missing.

HOME AS A PRECAUTION

He called in sick even though he wasn't really sick.

He spoke through a rag into the receiver and, insisting he was neither sick nor contagious, invited his boss to draw his own conclusions.

Must I stay home as a precaution against a more serious condition? Is this your professional opinion?

VIRULENT SEMIOTIC

The kids aren't kids anymore. They picket their graphic design department in protest of the Pitfire font, a typeface whose designer the MeToo movement has identified as predatory. His warm letters appear on signage, pamphlets, press kits, menus, mastheads, business cards, stationary, syllabi, course readers, fact sheets, FAQs, donor solicitations, wayfinding maps, and gold seal certificates throughout university life.

VARIATIONS ON KNOWING

I'm in a writing group called The Drunken Goats. But I don't drink, and I haven't seen any of my peers get too drunk. No, that's not true. I did watch one of us get pretty fucked up at our holiday party a few years ago. He grew very affectionate with everyone, and he passed out early, with his head in someone's lap. Before he went, though, he'd become obsessed with this sentence, the source of which no one has ever discovered:

> *The general known for sending his troops into the fray*
> *knowing full well that he would lose more of his own but*
> *with fewer overall casualties was a controversial warlord.*

He must have said it a hundred times, varying the diction and syntax with each articulation, his final utterances incomprehensible because he was slurring.

> *Understand, you, that she will lose women of her own*
> *but not those women she doesn't know to send into a fray*
> *anyway, before someone brands her Controversial Warlord.*

And now that I'm thinking about it, it wasn't a he-goat (Paulo, who is a loudmouthed drunk), but a she (Maggie, who is not). And she, for her love of fine art and prosodies marked by repetition and theme and variation, and for her performance that night, called to my mind Gertrude Stein (1874 -1946). Put another way: The goat who drank the most was like a High Modernist.

TIME PASSES

What is equivalent to a surprise party (for you!) attended by your best friends from each of your phases and a beam of light emanating from god knows where to sweep dark water, windows and crags of rock?

Answer: Imagine a novel like *To the Lighthouse*—one that begins with an afternoon and an evening, and accelerates, slowly at first, across lifetimes.

I don't want to run into anyone who I hadn't heard had remained behind. I wouldn't want to run into anyone who hadn't heard I'd stayed. May I not run into anyone in the darkness?

BY GEORGE (GOOD DAY)

My mother was the most beautiful woman I ever saw. All I am I owe to my mother. I attribute my success in life to the moral, intellectual and physical education I received from her. —George Washington

From a pair of Georges come two wonderful quotes, one from the novelist George Eliot, author of Middlemarch, and the other from the comedian George Carlin. "Affection is the broadest basis of a good life," says one. Says the other, "The day after tomorrow is the third day of the rest of your life." Can you guess who said which? I guess it's pretty obvious. Maybe it isn't important. They make a nice couple. No matter who said what, they make more meaning together than they do in isolation.

The poet George Oppen was a profound witness to the 20th century. As with my grandfather (George) on my mother's side, at the end of his rich life, Alzheimer's overwhelmed him. I learned then that when someone asks, "Where's my wife?" and he has no wife, you say, "She's not here right now" as a way of going along with the forgetting person's reality. You accept that nothing you do will bring back their ability to remember. You manage anxiety.

Back then, and finding them again now, I wrote the phrases 'profound witness' and 'disease of forgetting' in the margin beside the poet's lines,

> *And it is those who find themselves in love with the world*
> *who suffer an anguish of mortality...*

ENTRANCE OF THE GLADIATORS

The only adult performing in the recital loses his place on the page while he is playing. He puts his guitar down and, bowing his balding head to the audience, walks off stage sweaty and red and smiling. He's a beginner. This is his first recital. Sometimes his fingers stop moving. Because he works long hours as a high school teacher, he's had little time to practice. The music teacher, whose clientele, until the man showed up, consisted exclusively of children, stands in support of the man's effort, and soon the entire audience is applauding warmly. Having watched the music teacher rise, a boy peels away from his clapping mother and, climbing onto the stage, follows the man into the wings.

I don't know about this boy. I haven't decided yet. He may be obese or hyperactive. He may be all skin and bones. I'd love to connect the word frenetic with him. I love the idea of trouble-makers. He picks on kids by reminding them of their weaknesses. He makes us laugh with his fart noises. If not a troublemaker, he's an introvert with a slew of imaginary friends, a familiar on his shoulder. I haven't given much thought to how much of this is going to be autobiographical, but if he's going to sound like me he'll need to be simultaneously lonely and talkative. He wants to communicate something to you but doesn't know how to say it. He wants your attention. He'll talk your ear off if you let him. He fidgets. He grunts. He struggles to enunciate. His nasal passages are clogged all the time. His nose whistles.

He could be a million things really—the son of a banker, the son of a pilot, the son of a writer. He's a fatherless child. His mother works like a dog to give him music lessons. Or he has a brooding father. Or an effeminate one. He might have four older sisters or be sibling to his twin—a brother or a sister. I could easily make him adopted. Because I have an adopted sister in real life I could give him this characteristic with some authority. In fact, after I've finished this story I want to write a novel called The History of Adoption and dedicate it to Hong-Yen. My parents adopted her during the Vietnam War as part of a program known the world around as Operation Babylift. My own father is a veteran. In my History I will explore the connection between US military occupations and the adoption of orphans by American servicemen from the theaters of operation. My History will also profile famous adoptees throughout history—Daniel Boone, Dante Alighieri, Li Peng, Crazy Horse, John Lennon, Aristotle, Heracles, Bill Clinton, etc.

But I digress. Let's take it from the top. The boy could be obese, hyperactive, frenetic, constipated, lonely, dying of cystic fibrosis, verbal, oral, a thumb sucker, a break-dancer with a mean moonwalk, picky (finicky) eater, bully, son of banker, son of farmer, makes fart noises, familiar on his shoulder, tall for his age, small, average, towheaded, malnourished, quarterback for the Brown Bombers, future featherweight champion of the world, heavyweight champ, fly fisher, fascinated by piranhas, wearing braces, on the verge of mental illness, wrapped in a navy pea coat, collector of wheat pennies, collector of beer cans, Nike tennis shoes, a pair of topsiders, smart for his age, tough time enunciating, fidget, grunt, clear your throat, listen, elf, orc, demigorgon, the gay protagonist of Soehnlein's *The World of Normal Boys*, a devotee of Ferdinand the Bull, afraid of shapes made by moonlight, emboldened by the night, hanging from the eaves, lighting out, stepping through the cattails, tick on balls....

(You never know what memories you're going to trigger when you start digging. Once as a boy I discovered a bloated tick embedded in one of my testes. I was afraid to touch it and had to go the whole day—until my father got home—with it embedding further because only my mom was home and I didn't want her near my penis.)

...nose picker, dreams incessantly about caves, ties his own necktie, suffers from enuresis, self-administers insulin shot, fan of anime, animated, clairvoyant, the face of joy, skeptical of all holiday characters, of all holidays except birthdays, mostly skeptical of heaven, of heaven and hell, has sleep in his eyes, a strong swimmer, named after a constellation, sibling of a twin, practiced in the art of deadpan, a battle droid, graffiti artist, sketch artist, expert drawer of Porsches and Lamborghinis, one day dead of leukemia, encephalitis, computer whiz, geek, dork, afraid of heights, of dogs, of being left behind, being kidnapped, raspberries, titty twisters, being pinned down and tickled, greets all scorn with a smile, one day rapes or is raped, one day resuscitates an unconscious stranger, carries a pocket knife, an A student, pothead, daydreamer, a chip off the ole block, a real pistol, mama's boy, his father's son, a girl instead of a boy, somebody's sister, bilingual, itching to play ball, the last one picked, the first one picked, the grotesque, the sentimental favorite....

I now wonder if I needed to lose the thread of the story to understand how superfluous these possibilities can be. It's as if I needed to lose my way in order to discover the boy's function. Scanning the list I realize that I may introduce him by way of the tone of his voice, and in this way suggest that he is *precocious.*

The only adult performing in the recital loses his place on the page, puts his instrument aside, and hurries off the stage, humiliated. A boy from the audience follows him. He says: "Hey Mister, you got stage fright." Amused, the man replies, "What can I do about it?" "I have a switch in my head," explains the boy, "my anxiousness switch. I can turn it off whenever I feel like it. I'll show you in the second half of the program."

Later the boy walks on stage and, not much taller than his piano, takes a seat. "I will now play 'Entrance of the Gladiators,'" he announces, adding, with a wink to my protagonist, that he is quite nervous.

I wonder if you recognize this tune from its title. The man now waiting in the wings, 'my protagonist,' doesn't, but finds the title fitting from a boy who means to teach him about bravery. He thinks maybe it's a military march, and he's right. "Entrance of the Gladiators" is a military march written a long time ago for the calliope by a Czech composer whose name now escapes me. The man in the wings pictures chariots, chiseled chins, and battle-axes, only the tune's unmistakable association, as the boy begins, is not with gladiators, but with clowns. Think The Greatest Show on Earth. Think "Ringling Brothers Grand Entry." "Entrance of the Gladiators" is that tune to which too many clowns pile out of a tiny car. They arrive with cream pies, rubber chickens, and squirting flowers. They come in whiteface. They have bulbous noses. Long associated with circus sideshows and carnival midways prior to World War II, "Entrance of the Gladiators" is better known today as "Thunder and Blazes." This famous piece the boy plays on the piano flawlessly. He doesn't make a single mistake. Other kids follow him, playing such standards as "Greensleeves," "Twinkle Twinkle," and "Für Elise."

I had decided how this story was going to end before I started writing it, and now here we are at the end and I'm just not sure anymore. I had in mind a modern-day parable. I was going for something powerful. The man was supposed to peek out from behind the curtain to find the auditorium teeming with kids pressing their parents for fast food or something sweet to eat as they packed up their instruments. Pushing through the crowd to the boy with the anxiousness switch in his head, he was supposed to exclaim, "The most beautiful music in the world is hidden from us by its familiarity."

This simple phrase was both the seed of the story and my planned-for final sentence. I kept moving toward it, and would have reached it too, if I hadn't insisted on trying to choose a life for the boy. Then my parable got muddled. The idea of overly familiar music as nonetheless beautiful got lost because I couldn't leave you alone with the boy. I couldn't *enact* the moral of the story by allowing you to conjure him on your own. I had to get in there. I had to start yapping. I made a few preliminary decisions and, as if I could please everyone, proceeded to correct them, creating with my list an improvisation too idiosyncratic for my final sentence to truly ring.

Is it true? I just went back to my manuscript and deleted the list. I was surprised to find so many veiled confessions! I cut the story by two-thirds. No more enuresis. Or moonlit adventure. I removed all conjecture on my part, all traces of the real me. If I were a character you could say that I killed myself off. As the author, I've stripped the story down to my initial impulse: nondescript boy (precocious, stereotype) confronts nondescript man (stage fright, awkward new musician, aging) to teach him a valuable lesson. Now my concluding sentence is prominent and may make the hair on the back of your neck stand up. Or not. It's still not quite right. Something's still missing. I wish I could reinsert the list, the grunts, the orc, along with a few autobiographical details, maybe the bit about my adopted sister, just to make certain, but I've zapped all that information and am too tired to recreate it. I should at least try to get it back again. Otherwise I'll always wonder if my impetuous nature, even as it makes me cringe—makes me in my weakest moments want to run and hide and never speak again—is in reality a vital part of the story.

THE BOY FROM THURINGIA

My neighbor Wanda Czerwinski is a classical guitarist. Sometimes on a sunny Sunday she sits in her backyard and plays such stunning music as to make me forget the shirt I'm ironing or the egg I'm boiling or my own head throbbing. If in these tender moments I have my nose in a book, I blink and, gazing at the page, realize I've stopped reading. The fence separating our yard is too high for me to watch her perform. This is fitting because she is the most beautiful woman in San Francisco. Apropos of profoundest beauty, she's tangible like a melody is tangible. I must imagine her sitting in the sunshine with her guitar in her lap. I paint her long hair and long legs and nimble fingers in my mind in softest hues, to the accompaniment of her music.

I remember listening to Wanda one day while sitting in my kitchen polishing my shoes. Setting my rag aside, I looked at my hands, black with shoe wax polish and, losing myself in my hands and in the music, pictured myself standing outside a church called St. George's.

Placing my hands on the doors of my St. George's, I pushed my way inside to the sound of her music growing louder. Only it wasn't her guitar anymore. It wasn't Wanda. Someone was playing the organ. He or she was hidden from my sight. Like the rooftops and chimneys beyond Wanda's house, the grand pipes were all I could see of the organ. They climbed the walls of a distant gallery. Save for the organist, the church was empty. When the moment passed the church was gone. Wanda had stopped playing and, in what I must imagine as one fell swoop, had replaced her guitar in its case, snapped the case shut, and lapsed into silence.

Because she had been playing Bach's Violin Sonata No. 1, a masterwork in the guitar repertoire, I should pause here. I want to stop for a second before I say what happened next. This sonata is a major piece of music for both the violin and, in transcription, the guitar. I'm pausing to make it clear that I'm not inserting a famous score as the piece a woman plays in her backyard as some romantic effect. I'm not making this up. I'm not presenting Wanda as my muse as I begin to think about maybe hunkering down to one day possibly write—or at least contemplate the writing of—The History of Adoption. She really is this good at guitar playing. As far as I can tell, she is a world-class musician. She must be affiliated with some symphony somewhere, maybe the San Francisco Symphony, even if I haven't found her bio on the Internet. She plays in her backyard as if she were performing in some ancient concert hall in Europe. I suspect her of genius.

Similarly, I mentioned the mystery musician playing the organ in the imaginary church almost in passing. An organ in an empty church is not a quiet thing. Organ music is confrontational. The man playing the organ in my imaginary St. George's is Johann Sebastian Bach. I'm daydreaming about him not as an adult, but as the man he would become, from the perspective of what little I know about his childhood. St. George's is a church in Eisenach, the town in the county of Thuringia, where Sebastian was born, and not one of the churches where as an adult he composed the music the world knows him for. He was baptized in St. George's.

Imagine my surprise when I learned that he was orphaned at age nine and adopted by his eldest brother. I think if I could visit any time, place, or person as a way of inciting myself to write a vast history of orphans, I would sit with Sebastian one morning in Thuringia, soon after the death of his mother, but before his father's passing. In that time span—in the time of his orphaning—Sebastian, then an average student, was often absent from Lateinschule in Eisenach, where he received his primary education in religion and the humanities. I'd come to him in a moment when he was supposed to be at school but was instead sitting in his bedroom in his home on Fleischgasse. He of course wouldn't recognize me or know how to put me into words. But I would know him, and know what was in store for him.

I would remind him of his musical ancestry, beginning with his great-great-grandfather Viet Bach, trumpeter, lute player, violinist, who in the time of the Great Reformation fled Hungary to avoid religious persecution, and continuing with all the Bach cantors and organists and Town Musicians that Sebastian, after he'd married Magdalena and started a family of his own, would write about in his family history, "The Origin of Musical Bach Family."

I'd resist telling him about his future. I'd keep it to myself that his father, unaware of changes taking place in his body, was about to remarry, and that his stepmother would be abruptly widowed. I would not let on that his brother Christoph would soon thereafter adopt him and send him to the Lyceum in Ohrdruf, where he would continue his studies in, among other things, reading, singing, history, and natural science. I certainly would not say a word about his turbulent and itinerant career path as an adult. Or his children. Or the premature death of his first wife, and then his beloved Magdalena. I would keep to myself the date and cause of his own death, along with the future existence of the first violin sonata.

Against my own better judgment, fumbling my words, I would ask him something he could not possibly answer. How can I put this? In my moment with nine-year-old Sebastian, I'd somehow want to ask him what he thought was going to happen. Did he have some sense of how his mother's death had set his course? Could he feel his father's life winding down? At nine, did he sense the potential of his life growing inside him? Was he in some sense already writing his sonata? Was this moment a kind of Original Scene out of which all his music would flow? A first nudge in the awaking of his latent talent? (I ask this in part because his ability to master all aspects of playing and composition as a relatively young man is a mystery to me. It's not like he went to a music conservatory. I can find no record of a mentor. He learned scoring by copying the scores of the composers he admired. He was a self-taught fugist. I can see no clear path...).

As I was turning over in my mind my imaginary visit with Sebastian, the boy's father Ambrosius stopped him in their foyer and said, "Basti, what's that noise you keep making?"

Sebastian's hair was standing on his head like a blonde cabbage untucked in a breeze. He pressed his eyes together as if wringing out excess daylight and opened them again. He looked up. The spitting image of his father in his countenance and his dress, he gave a worried look. In his ruffled shirt and waistcoat—with his stockings pulled up over his breeches and gartered just below his knees—he was dressed like a miniature adult. He had no idea what his father was talking about. He asked, "What noise?"

But he was making a noise. Since his mother's death he'd gotten into the habit of grunting, if a grunt is what you'd call it. Imagine whispering the word "uh" every twenty seconds without realizing it. This is what it sounded like to Ambrosius: a gentle "uh" emanated from his boy. A pulse at regular intervals. Uh. The sound of someone sleeping fitfully through a bad dream.

"There it is again!" his father insisted. "You can't hear it?"

"Hear what?" asked Sebastian.

A disciplinarian prone to anger, his father had become much less direct in his demands and his instructions since the funeral. His tempering of his anger in the days, weeks, and months after the death of Elizabeth had turned that anger into a tender insistence. This noise must be his father's invention, one designed to break him of a new habit that he actually was aware of: he'd taken to talking out loud to his mother. He'd suddenly find himself asking her for advice or reenacting a conversation they'd once had. His father must have overheard them. Now he'd devised a method to train Sebastian to keep more to himself. "There it is again, Basti," he said. "You're making a noise like a wounded animal. It's simply impossible that you don't hear it."

"I swear, Father. I didn't say a word. I'm not talking to anyone."

Ambrosius turned from his boy and in a tone that would have been much sterner had Elizabeth survived, he said, "You're a boy, not a wounded animal. Instead of making that dreadful noise, why not study catechism? If you must make a noise make it not with your nose, your throat, and your mucus. Sing like Martin Luther."

Sebastian went away with the intention of keeping future conversations with his mother private. When he arrived in his bedroom he told his mother to leave him alone. A full moon shone through his window; like his mother's complexion when he imagined the things they said to each other, it seemed unusually detailed—close and clear in its luminescence.

He began sorting through his toys. In his hands he held a wooden toy hoop. Tossing the hoop in the moonlight, he made hoop shadows on his walls and on his floor and ceiling in many shapes and sizes. Waving his hand and his hoop all around, he imagined the shadows of bats and other flying things winging around his room. Then he set the hoop spinning like a coin and left it to wobble and wobble and fall over. He went to his desk and opened an iron box painted on the outside with portraits of Roman emperors and filled with inlaid tokens. He flung a toy soldier across the room, sent his comrades flying one after another. No pope would save them, just like no priest had assured his mother. Nothing he could do, not even becoming a monk, would be sufficient to merit his or anybody else's salvation. Only those who were predestined to receive divine grace would be saved. Had his mother been saved? How could he know? Who can know that he is among the chosen? Who can know if God will adopt him?

Soon Ambrosius began muttering hard to God through his trumpet, filling the house on Fleischgasse with brass. The sound sounded dead to Sebastian. Despite the magic of his box and the frontiers once crossed by his toy solders and the hoop through which bad things had always passed into good, all life had gone out of his belongings. He turned to the moon in his window. There was no moon. It was daytime. I heard the other kids of Eisenach running noisily by, underneath Sebastian's window, on their way to school. Among the racing children slow-stepping fowl burst into flight.

I wanted to see Sebastian running too. I wanted to put his big future on hold for a while. I sent him on his way. I had him grab his satchel and hurry downstairs. He kissed his mother. She was fine. He kissed his father. He was fine. I followed Sebastian as he charged onto the street, his heels clopping on stones, the wind in his ruddy face. In the shadow of Wartburg Castle, high on a hill, he ran past Town Hall with its tower trumpeters and the old Dominican monastery where the boys in the choir sang. He crossed the market plaza, stopping beside the statue of the famous dragon-slayer. I asked, "Wie heißt das Lied, das Sie gespielt haben?"—What is the name of the song I heard you play? "Ich stehe draußen von St. Georg"—I'm standing outside St. George's. "Ich warte in ihrem Schatten"—I'm waiting in its shadow.

The organ music I meant for Sebastian to hear at this moment wasn't organ music at all. It was Sunday afternoon and Wanda was playing Bach's sonata on her guitar again. My time with Sebastian was over. I got up from my kitchen table as I'd done a thousand times before when I wanted to have a word with Wanda. I'd only spoken to her once before, before I'd conceived my History. Before I knew anything about Sebastian or her guitar or what she looked like. Drawn by the scraping sound of a trowel, I'd spotted her between the slats in our fence. She'd been gardening. Japanese boxwood, rosemary, privet blooms. When I asked what she was doing, she said something in her thick Polish accent, something about a graft, something about a taproot, something about how gardening was a meditation. That was a long time ago. When she ever finishes playing, if I'm feeling courageous, I will go outside and reintroduce myself. I will tell her that she plays beautifully and leave it at that, when what I most want to say is that the music reminds me of sometimes solemn, sometimes joyous, oftentimes ardent, and always tumbling humanity.

THE EIFMAN BALLET IN BERKELEY

A performance of Anna Karenina.
The beauty of the production.
Anna's suicide.

On a personal note,
I remembered my happiness
of a few months ago
when I first got sober.

I said to more than one person,
"This is one of the happiest times in my life"
and feel a little funny about it.

Anna's rebirth as a pleasure seeker, cries Eifman
is expressed in the body's plasticity,
her death the consequence of denying
her child a mother's love.

Foreboding comes with my feeling
of not working hard enough.

MEMORIAL TO HARRY HAY (SILVER LAKE)

exit.
permanent
for
else
somewhere
bougainvillea
searching
bush daisies
spirits gone
dwork like
palm trees
the woo-
into
-
ows,
pine needles
shad-
apple tree
into the
ly to fade
passion flower
seem quiet-
scent of parents
bottle brush
gray figures, remini-
agave
Harry's approach, these
life will be dead soon. At
prickly pear
sider the most familiar people in your
needn't lose their urgency even when you con-
or let nature take it back. The exigencies of our lives
obscure ranch homes reminiscent of birdhouses. Prune it back
↓   Hay founded a Mattachine Society (1950). Where hills and groves
homosexuals." Engraved at the base of the Mattachine Steps, where Harry
"Giving votes in exchange for ideological support. To wit: identity polics for

In Los Angeles recently, my wife and I discovered in a plaque and a flight of stairs a memorial to the activist Harry Hay (1912-2002). He founded the Mattachine Society, probably the first gay rights group in the United States. Our poem, an elegy not unlike those stairs, seems to start on the ground and rise up.

A DRONE POEM FOR ROBINSON JEFFERS

As a teenager often mistaken for a stoner
self-medicating against his smash-mouth temper,
I built my own Tor House & Hawk Tower one feeling stone at
    a time,
while reading aloud the poems of Robinson Jeffers.
When thirty years hence my stoical gaze
once again fails to explain myself to a nosey onlooker,
I remove my glasses to wipe the crud out.

Dressed in black, I am not, I repeat,
I am not a High Valued Individual.
Seek not the heat in me with your Hellfire missile.
I mean only to pose a question to the purveyor of *Cawdor*—
O mournful widower of Hungerfield!—
whose tone I ape as a way of making myself feel worldly and
    cloistered—
in whose poem "The Machine" is stated,

> *The little biplane that has the river-meadow for landing-field*
> *And carries passengers brief rides,*
> *Buzzed overhead on the tender blue above the orange of*
>   *sundown.*

Innocuous at first glance,
the biplane is a new feature in the sky circa 1925.
In the unfolding poem it pushes aside,

...five troubled night-herons
turned short over the shore from its course, four east, one
northward.

II

At Crissy Field last Sunday, noontime in the 21st century,
L. Bielawa was performing her "Crissy Broadcast"
for fourteen ensembles—orchestral, instrumental, choral—
some eight hundred roving vocalists & players in all—
spirit children, each with something to pluck, pound, or
blow into—
when a civilian drone under real-time human control &
command
& with cameras for retinas & nostrils whirred by as naturally
as Jeffers's biplane trailing Lu Ban's magpie or the
Wright Flyer
in perpetuity across the top of the poet's pulpy ledger—

I don't know why, but lately the forms of things appear to me
with time
One of their visible dimensions.

In time, says he from his spot on the 20th century,
like the "thread brightness of the bent moon"
& human language fumbling the air,
with its seniors the night-herons, tumbling the air,
the biplane becomes *second nature...*

But what, Robinson Jeffers, would your drone poem portend
across a landscape of musicians and listeners commingled?
combined?

Children really, in a world at play?
Something buddhic or something, in your words,
"…crusted with blood & barbaric omens"?

Must all our inventions pass into nature?
Even those machines whose conscience resides
in remote locations? Our beholders? Their hovering eye
to shoot more than daggers? Or am I paranoid
in the face of clouds mounting outside my window,
while in the foreground lines & lines of passerines perch
  on wires?

Are these contraptions the same as any other, Mister Poet?
Or more like unbridled, unblinking power,
somehow supernatural or how might you say
          extranaturalis?

HERALD

1.

A friend asked me how to introduce dystopian fiction to teens. I like it in the context of social entrepreneurship: how are young people actually addressing the big problems drama-tized in futuristic fiction about now? Must Octavia Butler and George Orwell be right all the time?

2.

Now the quietest among them has announced that he will be named editor-in-chief of a newspaper in a postapocalyptic coun-try. This is remarkable for several reasons. One is that in his speech he sounds panic-stricken. Two: He truly believes the end is near. Three: He assumes that the social structure afterwards will be tribal. Four: We're already seeing an end to newspapers. Number five is his conviction that he (of all people) will not only survive but also be elevated to a position he is unqualified for in current society. Imagine a bellhop with hardly a high school education becoming an editor-in-chief after the world has ended. But let it be so, if for no other reason than the boldness of his vision and the charm that is the naiveté of daydreamers.

DINNER SCENE

'There's a lot to work out here,' wrote the dad in his Yelp review, 'unless you like everything well done extremely pricey.' Though the crudo and baby gems had been awesome starters, his boy's Monster Burger, avowedly medium, reminded everyone of charcoal. Despite his wife's nice crispy skin, the fish everyone agreed was inedible. To top it all off, not only did the place dish up bland lentils, but their butts were cold on steel ice chairs and, on what passes here for a winter's night, there were no space heaters. Looking on the bright side, his muscles were passable on the half shell and it's always great to dip assorted burnt meats into the tangy sauce of someone else's cooking. This came at the end of the meal, after the fam had picked through what it could stomach. Only then did the waitress ask, "Did we leave room for dessert?" After a long pause, the dad pointed out a fig panna cotta too dense for chewing. How generous he'd felt giving the experience two stars on the car ride home.

The response was swift. 'To start,' wrote the restaurant owner, 'we're probably not the place for you, but that you were visibly upset when you arrived, ranting about icy cold seats on our hottest day in memory. Honestly,' he went on to say, 'we were all concerned about you. Your condition seemed more mental than physical. We worry that you are not a stable parent.' The rest was history, with its winners and its losers. On behalf of his entire crew, he congratulated the dad on this attempt at constructive criticism. Not an easy thing to do. 'We should all be so helpful in these contentious times, while not fighting too hard for what we believe in.'

Concerning the restaurant owner's response, the husband and wife must agree to disagree. For him, the customer was always right. The restaurant owner must act like his own best waitperson. The dad downgraded it to a one-star experience. Evocative of needy parents and hardened capitalists, obsequiousness as a rule bugged the crap out of the mother. A duel would have been better. To shoot and be shot in the eyes of your child. Ha! But seriously folks, she would have preferred the men confront each other face-to-face instead of writing about it on the Internet. You can never take it down. You must check it dozens of times a day to see if you've gained any admirers. You must watch your husband play out the dinner scene again and again, making an archenemy of a guy in a chef's hat who is his equal in pride and manner. It will never be over with.

SENTENCES WRITTEN AT SAINT COLUMBA'S CHURCH

Praying he once read is a pioneering form of picketing, a revolutionary thing to do, like the walkout, the sit-in, or leaving your weight dead in the hands of a kettling army.

Out back of a chapel, and in with the fields, forest, the living hedges, a blouse lay in a wad. Reaching for it, he hears the sea. The chill air and the arc of the sky give the color blue to the smell of fennel.

The blue blouse is a boy's blouse from a bygone era whose cheery bugs live in its folds. Whose lifespans we may measure in hours, minutes, and seconds.

A breeze catches in the cypresses. A blouse caught in a sea of nettles. Pick it free. Flap it open. Feline beetles upwell in the thousands. Like a flipbook animating a trotting mare or a sprinter in an Olympiad, the benevolent swarm renders his silhouette as a flickering Vitruvian Man.

Seen from afar through an ocular window, his silhouette shows not his taking communion but his talking it over with himself: "I'm not hungry enough to eat something," he reasons. "But I could be okay with the ritual of it, once I got it into my system."

Think of something you do everyday and swap it out for protest.

Praying, he reads, is a pioneering form of picketing. He prays in the morning for the courage to wave a sign in the face of captains of industry late one afternoon.

Ladybugs pelt like kisses and like the touch of a kiss they dissipate. The climate is changing.

CRIME SCENE

A neighbor recounts having survived a home invasion. The perps broke an arm and a leg, and they gave him a severe concussion. This was no movie. Their masks weren't of celebrity politicians. He realized they were wearing masks only after he understood each downcast face to replicate the other.

To write the story of the murder of a neighbor, she will interview a man who, complicit if not guilty, is on his way over. She must abdicate the knowledge that makes her our author. She must play it cool, beginning right now by not jumping every time headlights sweep the window.

See gore at its most vicious. The setting, a city block. The perp, an incel. The victims, call girls, miss their mothers' milk. "Extreme violence," argues the director, "bespeaks the brokenness of a community." Public outcry for moderation gives the picture its retro coloration.

ANGLO SAXON RIDDLE

manna	blurt	god
grab	man	untold
lamb	gonad	runt
litter	dragon	nut
brat	almond	gun
bond	nomad	lung

FEEDING

When out of the blue the child asked what the difference was between homicide and suicide, she cried, "You're spilling!"—and would he please hold his cup upright. When he asked if suicide was more common than homicide, or if homicide was more common between the two, she said, "You're getting all wet!—please hold your cup upright, or if the next time you're thirsty how about I don't feed you?"

THE ABCS OF MURDER

An amorphous assassin—say, *you*, or someone *like* you, so
    rude, so crafty—must

Be, or rather the murder itself must be (sorry for sounding so
    accusatory! it's my nature) iron-

Clad in its weave of the original scene—whodunit?—with the
    word on the tip of my tongue,

Dénouement. As for the yoking yarn hung between broken
    home and home reformed, it must be

Efficacious, this yarn, a quality neither too meek nor too
    strong for an old-fashioned mutilation, one

Framed and named for you—Alain (Alun) Goodberry—
    unless I change your name on the basis of say

Gender to something like Elaine as a means of dipping my
    stick into you know what:

Honey. After all, who doesn't bring heat to the molasses of
    male and female organs?

I mean *really* bring it, especially now that you've filched a
    perfectly good piano wire from a perfectly good piano and

Jotted down your demands not in blood but in a font of

cutthroat letters, each (demand, that is, not letter) in

Keeping with your sense of humor: No two are distinguish-
able from each other. Ha! How I love, really

Love you, Mr. or Mrs. Goodberry. You kill an innocent by
severing her or his carotid artery,

Manufacture a list of demands a hundred items long that
amounts to a single demand made time and again, and

Never once explicating the nature of this demand, go about
your business as if you hadn't already

Opened the throat of your hostage, not once stopping to
think hey maybe he or she is worthless as a cadaver!

Please do tell me, Mr. or Mrs. Goodberry: How could you be
so shortsighted as to inflict this Eternal

Quietus—with wire or bare hands or bare bodkin, or what-
ever one does it with—before collecting

Ransom from our mutual enemies, the Headlongs and their
insufferable neighbors, the Rutherfords?

Sophomoric is not too small a word for you, unless there's
genius hidden in your hundred-headed demand

That I, a little thick at times, can't comprehend. So help me
out here, you introverted hermaphrodite. Explain your

Ultimatum: *To see your special someone alive again you must sacrifice a red roan upon the Altar of Man*, plus

Verification via home video to capture both the equine's writhing and—O ad hoc ritualists!—your playacted keening,

Wailing, really, not for horse but for victim, when a feminine form emerges, a mother figure scripted as a manful

Xanthippe, to recount for the camera her slain offspring's biological milestones—say teething—all the while

Yearning for the wandering horse to wander once again and, capering at noon, to epitomize the sun at its

Zenith when, sans the corroboration shadows for assassins extend, bloodletting grows inopportune, nonextant.

[No Gadfly]

I've always wanted to tell my story about horses and maybe even write it down. Before I knew what (of what had happened) I would emphasize, and what I would let go of, I thought wouldn't it be cool to begin with that famous quote from Plato's *Apologia*, when Socrates, soon condemned to death for his subversive teaching (of youth), compares the state that would execute him to a horse and himself, or course, to a gadfly. Thank God I realized in [the nick of] time how pretentious this would have been. It had nothing to do with nothing, let alone me. I hate the idea of anyone thinking me pretentious. I'd rather die. No Socrates, no horse, no gadfly.

HEAD

[oil on canvas]

dragon
flies
figure
prominently
or
more
or
less
tangentially
in
the
lives
    &Today isn't the day.
times   Trust me.
    I've made many plans.
of   Please don't stop me.
men   Think of the people around us.
    &Yes, you can have my head today.
women   But if you wait until tomorrow
living   you can have it then
    and also keep your own head about you.
in   Take your hands out of your pockets.
every   Walk away.
epoch   Walk away.
ever
written
down
about
human
emotion

THE PLACE IN THE PICTURE

The woman in the other room is a grandmother.   A
grandson watches a grandmother from darkness through a
lit door.   A grandson knows nothing about a grandmother.
A grandmother arrived unceremoniously to a grandson who
she has never met before.   The articles here confuse inti-
macy.   Though no one is heartless, this isn't a feel-good
situation where everyone is at odds with everyone at first but
eventually finds in the other a kindred spirit.   This
is a story of complete hardness between a mother and a
daughter.   A son who is a grandson must navigate the
ancient rift between a daughter who is a mother and a mother
who is a grandmother in a moment before leaving home to
work for the Peace Corps in Botswana.   A grandson must
not dig up the past.   A grandson fears not so much the
person of a grandmother, who stands barely five feet tall and
more often than not is lost in a daydream, as he does her tem-
per.   When she speaks to him he feels held at gunpoint.
A mother has a similar effect on a son.   A grand-
son feels obliged to love a grandmother he has never spent
time with.   One essential question is, 'How can a grand-
son not know a grandmother?'   This is one of the
essential questions a son won't ask a mother.   Another
is how a mother comes to have so much power.   A
grandmother orders a grandson around like she has always
lived there. She makes him rewash all the dishes when she
finds a spot on one. She browbeats him into pounding out
rugs with a broom or the pavement.   He must do not
only his own laundry but also launder such fabrics of the
common areas as curtains, slips, and covers.   A grand-

son and a grandmother both have deviated septa.   If
there is one way for them to commiserate with each other,
a way more intimate than the rote cues they follow, it is a
willingness to talk about nasal cycles.   To talk about their
noses brings smiles to their faces.   A grandmother
smiling is a major event for a grandson to witness. A son
tells a mother in private.   If a grandmother wishes
she could just leave sometimes, why not just leave sometimes?
If a grandmother adores color and figures, why not join an
artists' studio for the senior citizens?   A mother
asks a son to ride the bus with a grandmother to the rec cen-
ter in the evening.   A grandmother with an evening
activity needs a chaperone to arrive safely.
A grandmother makes a seascape one week and a herd of
wild horses the next.   She paints a
herd of mustangs from a photograph in a book that belongs
to her instructor.   She paints halved apples and pots of
flowers.   A grandson looks at these pictures and thinks
he wouldn't mind having one.   A grand-
son thinks they might be worth something to someone.
          Because she finds other artists at the artists' studio for
the elderly insufferable, a grandmother paints one last still
life, a view from a hilltop looking down upon the valley town
in northern Italy where she was born, and puts her brushes
away forever.   A grandmother claims she's put
her brushes away forever but it isn't forever.   No one is
lying but acting out emotion.   A grandson sitting
in darkness watches a grandmother through a lit doorway.
She stands before the painting she calls "Asiago" with a brush
in one hand and a palette of colors in the other.
          She touches it up as it hangs there, framed on
the kitchen wall. He doesn't speak but jots down the chang-
es she makes on the graph paper he used to use to diagram
traffic flow on the streets of his neighborhood.
          He watches her painting over portions of her picture

with things that could logically go there.　　　　　Their
routine will go on like this for days and weeks and months,
until the day he leaves for Africa.　　　　　He
writes what's missing and what's new to the situation across
the grid of his paper as if his words and phrases, like places
and objects in the physical world, have fixed coordinates,
we'll take the bus ride into the hills
follow the bridge out of this city
roll out on a morning like any other

my things are ready

hung on her wall otherwise bare
slopes foot the room for so long
hills not a thing like the ones first painted

set above our misplaced couch
a bowl of cloth flowers
a hat rack
plates in glass

even the cloth flowers

she sets up a fresh canvas every now and again
never makes a mark
I used to ask

I don't ask her that anymore

last year the far away rectangles
the little patches of land
I noticed more yellow
a new cloud hung in the sky
a small house appeared on the horizon
I don't know where these people come from

all blank except one

it's getting darker

I still can't explain the sun

running my hand over the brown hills
I remembered them green
and new shadows fell over ones there before
before the sun which today shines gray

or doesn't shine at all

LONELINESS

If only for a second
I swear to God
we were the same person

○

except that I was a
white guy from Shawnee Mission   lonely

ylenol
and he was a
new American, born in Nagasaki.

lonely

ereht dnoces a roF
doG ot raews I
nosrep emas eht erew we

a saw I taht tpecxe
noissiM eenwahS morf yug etihw
ylenol a saw eh dna
.ikasagaN ni nrob naciremA wen

lonely

73

TOLD ON A MOUNTAIN

I do comedy because though I am rarely depressed I am always disappointed.

I do comedy because for my day job, a soul-less job, I manage a database.

I do comedy because my colorblindness causes mismatched outfits.

I do comedy because I am both avuncular and childless. Rather, my wife and I don't have children, and I am uncle-like, and she is a hoarder.

I do comedy because my wife collects a lot of stuff but not enough for anyone to compare her to an installation artist like Robert Rauschenberg. She would need to specialize in a medium like synthetic surfaces and really put her mind to it.

I do comedy because on Saturday mornings, when my wife referees kids' soccer games, she runs backwards with a whistle in her mouth as quickly as I can run forward.

I do comedy because my wife's demand for a divorce is our in-joke. She doesn't really want one. It's just something she says. It's funny. Freud tells us that a good joke reminds us of what we're afraid of. I do comedy because my wife is an armchair Freudian.

I do comedy because I must clean the mirror in my bathroom every Saturday morning and again on a weekday. I sit on the toilet and, looking up from my book, say of every streak, 'Not on my watch.'

I do comedy because I am horse-faced. One pokes fun at his own lantern jaws.

I do comedy because I suspect everyone of laughing at me. I respond to their laughter by getting out in front of it.

Once you're out in front of it, you can turn and face it head-on. You raise your hands as if in surrender and talk to it in a forceful and lighthearted manner.

I do comedy because along with my colorblindness come uncontrollable eye movements.

I do comedy because as a little boy and an older boy my mother couldn't keep her hands off me until one day when I knocked her to the ground.

I do comedy because I see my mother once every other December.

I do comedy because I am incapable of keeping a secret. 'Loose lips sink ships' is the adage they used against me. It always struck me as sexual. It was Helen of Troy and it wasn't her mouth we were talking about.

I do comedy because my practice of prayer and meditation amounts to a few minutes of stillness followed like a kid by fidgeting.

I do comedy because as a child, before it was talked about, before social media provided virtual proving grounds to antagonists like mine, and before webinars showed parents and teachers true interventions, I was bullied. My bully, who shall remain nameless (Wexler), waits for me on the street corner I spend my energies circumnavigating. When he gets his hands on me, he will rub my face in the dirt. He will steal my money. He will call me a mamas' boy and a faggot. He turns me into what they used to call a truant when, to stay in bed, I convince my mother that I have a mysterious illness.

I do comedy because in middle age I wore braces. This is less about orthodontics and more about the poverty of my upbringing.

I do comedy because I cheat on my taxes. I cheat on my taxes because I'm not funny enough to be audited.

I do comedy because I am always on time and never a minute late. I have some serious questions for those who are always late.

I do comedy because I believe in angels. They arrive in time to help me with my punch lines. They are the source of my originality. In the guise of my sense of humor, they are my great defender.

ORNITHOPHOBIA

At the age of forty, he met a woman and at long last began to feel himself falling in love. In the past, his fear that a prospective lover would spurn him for his flaws and the secrets he was keeping always started off small and grew into his own conclusion that they were all wrong for each other.

Learning now that the woman who had so completely captivated him was a bird lover, he remembered a moment from his childhood when, walking through the shady mission, a blackbird swooped down from some perch somewhere and, flapping in his ears, pecked and squawked, chasing him all the way to safety. When he described a bird with yellow eyes, a purple head, and greenish wings and body to his mother, a bird lover herself, she told him that the Brewer's blackbird was extremely territorial.

As a day didn't pass when he didn't think about his mother, he today wondered if maybe she would have accepted this new girl, if only for their mutual love of the bird kingdom. Though he missed her badly, he was also glad that she wasn't around to tell his lover of the terror her boy felt when even the most majestic of fliers passed over. She had never had the best timing, and always managed to say the kinds of things that ruined his chances of ever finding somebody.

GILDA'S CLUB

1.

Wandering amid the women in his life, a once-lonely man with a wry sense of humor found love simply by persisting in telling the same dumb jokes over and over again—and listening for laughter. Lifting her veil, he now tried to speak, but found himself speechless in the eyes of the wisest comedienne he'd ever witnessed.

2.

American comic Gilda Radner (1946 -1989) wore many faces. One she called Roseanne Roseannadanna. She played other characters with names like Brungilda, Emily Litella, Candy Slice, and Judy Miller.

Donning a huge head of tight curls, she, Roseanne Roseannadanna, was a fake and movingly puerile consumer-affairs reporter on the mock news broadcast on the late-night variety show *Saturday Night Live*—first airing in the early 1970s.

Brash and tactless, she, Roseanne Roseannadanna, was quick to savage colleagues and viewers alike—anyone who got in the way of what she was saying—before digressing into something bodily, something scatological, like her own flatulence or the status of one of her nose hairs.

She, Roseanne Roseannadanna, dropped names so that in one

moment she was reading a letter from a viewer, usually one Mister Feder of Fort Lee, New Jersey, asking about quitting smoking or how breast feeding a baby works in practice, and in the next she was going on about her supposed run-in with Princess Grace of Monaco.

Maniacal, sarcastic, insistent, she, Roseanne Roseannadanna, marked my earliest exposure to this kind of playacting. As a form of insistence, she, Roseanne Roseannadanna, chronically referred to herself by her full name. Save for the emphatic I, she favored fewer pronouns for herself when speaking about herself, of whom she spoke admiringly.

Though she, Ms. Radner, was a master of sketch comedy, none of the teenagers in my life have ever heard of her. This makes sense. It would be like my reciting Lucille Ball when I was their age or a teenager forty years hence laughing at the antics of I don't know who or what in our present moment.

Once Ms. Radner was diagnosed with ovarian cancer, she famously said, "Having cancer gave me membership in an elite club I'd rather not belong to."

Upon her death, her husband, also a famous comic, helped to found Gilda's Club, an international organization created to support people living with cancer.

Having sworn off marriage after the death of his wife Gilda Radner, the widower did eventually remarry. Sometime after that—or was it sometime before?—he sought therapy. For what specifically, I don't know. Loneliness? Anger? Depression? Impulsivity? He said to his shrink something like, Hey Doc, I have the urge to give away all my money. Well, replied the therapist, how much money do you have? Me? he said, I owe $300.

One day I was walking down Division Street in Nashville when I happened upon a red brick building—home to one the chapters of Gilda's Club. So read the bronze plaque on the facade on such a bright and muggy day. The parking lot was empty. The windows were dark. Cupping my hands about my face to peer through the glass, I got the sense of a clock ticking. Dust motes. Empty chairs. Dusky silence. A card table stood strewn with magazines. A turntable sat beside a stack of records. Beyond bookshelves, a view to a kitchen and, everywhere, jutting shadows. Suddenly overwhelmed by a sense not so much of time passing as of time having passed—of not so much death as the insignificance of a single life in the context of the sheer number of individuals who have entreated youth to linger—I backed away from the window and, looking around to see if my nosiness had raised eyebrows, I buried my hands in my pockets and, with a down-turned gaze, continued my walk as if nothing had happened.

CLOSE-UPS HURT COMEDY

While I shoot blanks and you age out, the complicated circus car chugs the ring, throwing up spare parts like girls tossing underclothes over a boudoir screen.

In an epigram for you, my bride, my confidante, always the avid reader, Nabokov reminds us that the difference between the comic side of things and the cosmic side depends upon a single sibilant.

We're standing in the aisles when our whey-faced planet, swathed in the Human Mop, goes whirring by, giving way to a gorilla named Peter the Great, his flatulent elephant filling the room after our planet's sudden departure and, all but invisible to the naked eye, decked out in rococo tusks by happy-go-lucky prop men.

Soon the Buddhists are filing in and, in violation of the ground rules for any good walking meditation (silence!), talk about themselves in the third person.

Paul's knocked off his mule on his way to Damascus and discovers God.

Because the comic side isn't always funnier, flying men remind us, when we go through the air, to use our heads as a rudder.

Thank Steve I'm a funny writer; if not for him, my closest friend in life, I'd still be stuck in my old job, doctoring obits.

I can't be funny.

On the road home, we train our gaze on the nighttime sky: Venus shines brightly just before the break of dawn, the Seven Sisters close in on the red star Aldebaran.

Recounting to each other the death-defying acts we've witnessed, I joke that when I die you bury me with our ticket stubs.

Our old debate ensues: I say you'll live longer and you remind me that mine are the genes of centenarians, and for the first time ever, you say in a way that reeks of codependence that you want to go first, because you can't bear the thought of being alone.

If you do die first, I conjecture, it will be the most profound experience of my life.

[Silence.]

Coming to light, the deep dark secret I might be happier on my own isn't the only one I'm harboring: Every time the show gets over I never imagine the road home without you.

I love you—I love your company!

TIME SPACE CAPSULE

In an age of tell-alls, exposé & everybody's autobiography, it wasn't so much his disdain for confessions traded in the marketplace in Manhattan at the expense of a mother or husband's privacy, or more broadly the first-person singular I, seeming always to collapse into solipsism, call it navel-gazing, as it was the overwhelming sensation of being left out of a conversation.

"Where but in the nighttime sky," he asked, "is my rarefied public? Who are you, my reader? What of mine is worth describing?" That a memoir worthy of our times, the kind he lusted after writing, had universal appeal—this was his litmus test: "What of homo sapiens will it reveal to an extraterrestrial?"

Such a manuscript was the Library of Alexandria encoded on a microchip, an astronomical clock signaling rotation rates of pulsars, a drop of human blood encased in a diamond, the DNA of the human genome etched into one of its facets.

Only at the advent of his physical decline, the onset of Parkinson's, did a new literacy bloom inside. Only then did habits of mind embedded even in his grocery list mirror, in the midst of its casualties, the architecture of the diamond.

LOW TIDE

Once at Point Reyes Station
I bought a kite
a big diamond-
shaped number no
that's not right.
I remember
I'd changed my name
rather my mind
and at the last second
chose something boxy
with panels.

Almost in the same breath
I bought two shirts at a shop
at the opposite end of town
the long blocks
notable for low buildings
high curbs and the rain
water running in the gutters.
I told the woman
who sold me the shirts
one plaid, one solid
about kites hanging from rafters,
the shopkeeper whom she knew
as a friend of her late husband
and my selection process
once I'd committed myself
to making a purchase.
She asked me my name.

I told her in a startled voice
it started with a J
because I needed at least a finger
hold on the truth
to speak without blenching
adding that mine was a quiet life
on the verge
so I'd always felt
of transformation.

Eyeing my kite
she announced my boyhood
for I was a boy
as far as she could tell
trapped inside a man's body
as erupting.

I'd chosen a stickless parafoil.
Something less boxy
than I'd previously let on
the diamond-shaped one
complete with two
beautiful streamers.
The woman who sold me the shirts
a thin ruddy haired woman
with large green eyes
and a penchant for sighing
nodded without speaking
and over time
and with downcast eyes
blurted nouns like whitewash
and mackerel sky
between silences.
A specimen of her (late) stage of life
and old enough to be my mother

she was in magnificent physical shape
and numbingly isolated.

At the beach with Janet
for she had closed up shop early
I scrawled for her
on the sky
with my parafoil.
Wind whipped her face.
The hem of her coat flapped
about her kneecaps.
Waves petered out at our feet
after their proverbial crashings.
Following the kite with her eyes
she asked me what
I did with myself.
Besides scholarship, I said
for I was a Sunday Gogol scholar
partway to learning Russian
I was writing something
based on sound
something forgiving both of illogic
and running against the grain
of my character
typographical errors.
Stacking her hands
atop her sternum
as if to clutch a medallion
she nodded her head
in the affirmative
her long quilted coat
a patchwork of squares
enumerating a spectrum
of colors I tend to call
autumnal.

In the first place
liquid darkness reads like a womb.
(The rapid cycling parent of origin
composes four episodes a year.
I'm talking about madness
when the clock secretes liquid.
We secret it [sic.] in the dark,
when we think it's night.
We don't understand
the kind of sleep we'd have
if we didn't have electric lights.)

In the second place
Janet, whose name,
an English diminutive of Jane,
female equivalent of John,
finds its roots in Yochanan
the Yahweh of the grace of god—
my friend, a stranger of mine
Janet rises into the air and the light.

In the third place
is the life of the imagination.

ABOUT THE AUTHOR

David Booth is a high school humanities teacher and a poet. He lives in San Francisco, California, with his wife Ingrid Hawkinson. His blog is sacredpedestrians.com. *Too Bright to See* is his debut collection of poems.